CW00531109

Wisdom
and
Wit

Wisdom and Wit

301 Gems to Grow
and Grin

Shanti Rose

Turquoise River Publications

ISBN (paperback): 978-1-959965-00-8
ISBN (ebook): 978-1-959965-01-5)

Library of Congress Control Number: 2022921778

First printing 2023

Cover and Interior Design: Turquoise River Publications

 Published by Turquoise River Publications

Turquoise River Publications
4315 50th Street NW
Suite 100 P--MB 7034
Washington, DC 20016

For inquiries, visit our website: turquoiserp.com

Introduction

In these swirling times, as energies bounce with unexpected speed, we need wisdom to hold onto and wit to lighten our load.

Here in these pages, you will find the very messages you need.

Dedication

This book is dedicated to beloved humanity.

May we expand our love and come together as friends.

1.

Life is an amazing journey. Sometimes we
exclaim WOW, only to be followed by YIKES
in the next scene.

2.

Two tangling octopi muddy the water.
That's what angry energy resembles
when people argue and fight.

3.

Having an opinion about everything
is a tiring trait.

4.

About diet: Put forth great effort to avoid
meals of self-belittlement.

5.

A poor attitude can be compared to dirty
laundry piled in a heap.

6.

Some personalities dissect their problems down to the bare bones. They peer into every possibility until the debated pros and cons make them sick.

7.

Develop a good-finding nature rather than being a fault-finder.

8.

Continual thoughts of resentment are similar to a woodpecker that *tap — tap — taps* a dead tree!

9.

Allow no one to make you feel flawed.

10.

Sometimes, all that's needed to reset our balance button is a nice afternoon nap.

11.

People want a dose of cheerful you.

12.

Form good habits and work to eliminate patterns that are foreign to love.

13.

A timid person never accomplishes much.

14.

Our earth journey: to increase our love while renovating bad traits.

15.

A morose person is not an uplifting acquaintance.

16.

Meddling in the doings of others
is a non-advantageous sport.

17.

The rule of life: Be good, do good.

18.

Timeless wisdom: Whatever we believe,
we create.

19.

It is wise to wear steel-toed shoes when
you're near those who don't care if
they step on your toes.

20.

Refuse to be hard on yourself over a misstep.

Correct your thinking and jog on.

21.

Life whirls with uncompromising speed until a conscious effort is made to downsize activities.

22.

Life is a solitary journey in
the midst of a crowd.

23.

The past is over; the future has
not been revealed.

Live in the present moment and be happy.

24.

We are only required to do our best
at any given moment.

25.

Acceptance is the route to comfortable living.

26.

Life invites us to adjust to changing scenes.

27.

The great miter box of life fits events together
perfectly for our education.

28.

We meet those who teach us valuable lessons.

29.

We are given many choices. We swim in the
ripples of these choices in times ahead.

30.

The magnifying glass of inner scrutiny locates
patterns foreign to love and brings them
to the surface for renovation.

31.

The only creed is love.

32.

The sweet voice within is always urging us to live in love.

33.

The only way to change our circumstances is through love.

34.

Each person has a story to tell about their life. Each story is unique, yet the theme is the same — learning to love.

35.

When we are kind-hearted and loving, we feel happy.

36.

If you desire peace, forget about yourself.
Think: *I want to help someone today.*

37.

Love and give, give and love. That is the way
to create a fantastic society.

38.

Remind yourself: Giving up is not
in my owner's manual.

39.

An affirmation: I am successful
in everything I do.

40.

Angry people need to live inside
their heads. Never easy!

41.

An optimist expects the best; a pessimist fears the worst.

42.

Just when a situation becomes too hot to endure, a cooling breeze comes in.

43.

Find one person to encourage today. That person may be you.

44.

Seek balance in disruptive times.

45.

Differences of opinion are fine as long as they are not laced with violence.

46.

The mind wants instant resolution.

Life does not work that way. We take
one step, then another.

47.

Each day is best navigated with
a thankful spirit.

48.

The greatest prayer is one of gratitude.

49.

The tapestry of a beautiful life is woven
with threads of kindness.

50.

Injure no one in thought, word, or action.

51.

Life is a university. We learn many lessons
through pleasant and irksome interactions.

52.

Soar to the highest heights
with an optimistic spirit.

53.

Unkind acts are hatched in a nest of jealousy.

54.

Rise to the challenge of being okay
with what is lost.

55.

One cannot live happily if vain, deceitful,
or rude behavior is followed.

56.

If darts of hostility are sent your way,
walk away and have a sunny day.

57.

Angry outbursts and thoughts of retaliation
create a simmering pot of sickening stew.

58.

Anger is a wildfire out of control. It destroys
relationships in its path.

59.

Anger swirls internally like blades of a fan,
sending poison into every cell of the body.

60.

Learn to excise fear with the precision of
a surgeon and the power of a saint.

61.

When one lives under the influence of fear,
what is least desired is set in motion.

62.

A good laugh is a stress-buster.

63.

Become aware of your thoughts. Change the
station if you don't like the tune.

64.

Think well.

Thoughts create the future.

65.

The diet of the mind creates a climate
of peace or distress.

66.

Every loving thought embraces the
whole world in cordial warmth.

67.

Rise above a powerless state. You can move
a mountain with your thoughts.

68.

Thoughts turn into words; words
become actions; actions invite challenges
or a smooth road ahead.

69.

If we encourage each other, we can massage
the days of tomorrow into a better attitude.

70.

Let the violin of your soul continue to play
sweet music, even when the instruments
of others are out of tune.

71.

Think of your feet as transporters of
a vehicle that radiates love.

72.

If life were always easy, we would become
inactive blobs of complacent matter.

73.

There is strength in silence; much can
be gained through composure.

74.

Avoid getting mad at someone who is mad at
you. A double-mad is difficult to unlock!

75.

Let pain from the past decompose
in the warm soil of forgiveness.

76.

Everyone sings their own tune.

Each song is different and unique.

Practice harmonizing with others.

77.

The more possessions we own, the more effort
it takes to polish their chrome.

78.

Petite-minded individuals like to argue
over diminutive issues.

79.

If the world's people were given only
one instruction, it would be to become
a rose without the prickly thorns.

80.

We cannot change the mind of another person.
Yet, the vast majority tries.

81.

Gratitude opens the flow of abundance,
whereas greed constricts prosperous returns.

82.

Shine brightly, despite gray skies.

83.

Stress comes from an accumulation
of unloving thoughts.

84.

The beautiful dance of life needs
only to be appreciated.

85.

You can bathe in the vast sea of wisdom
after you have learned to stay afloat
in troubled waters.

86.

A ten-ton ego is a heavy weight to carry.

87.

A mere pin-prick can deflate a pumped-up ego.

88.

It is a short road from being cocky
to having to cope!

89.

On moods: Remain happy and let others
deal with their own thunder.

90.

Black moods are potholes on the road
of life. Hit one, and you will get a flat tire
that places your happiness on pause.

91.

Lack of respect for others is a lack
of respect for yourself.

92.

Stay optimistic! Just when you think
the night will never end, dawn breaks.

93.

Be careful not to exaggerate.
Tall tales are actually lies.

94.

The unwilling to see, won't.

95.

Follywood is home to many people.

96.

Focus on the good that is happening rather than the dim view of those who hold distorted imaginings.

97.

Dead-end streets are just that.

98.

Words of encouragement bring smiles to sad faces.

99.

After a tough experience, one either becomes bitter or better.

100.

You are over-qualified to navigate the experiences of your life successfully.

101.

Experiences talk loudly. They leave little room for debate.

102.

Some experiences are tough.
Each experience is a perfect educator.

103.

A perspective: The refugee camps are full.

Do you have it so hard?

104.

We keep riding the merry-go-round of painful experiences on the same theme until we get the meaning.

105.

Life is not a battle; it is a journey
through needed experiences.

106.

Would you make the same mistake again?
If not, you have changed.

107.

Just a question: Are your credit cards
on life support?

108.

Purchase only what you can afford.

109.

I have a simple comment about braggarts:
They can be all that until they're not.

110.

Children are great teachers. As parents, we only
wish they would let us up for air occasionally.

111.

On raising teenagers: Sometimes our opinion
only counts in our own opinion!

112.

Running after desires is like a cat chasing
its tail — amusing but pointless.

113.

Desires often speak louder than common sense.

114.

When one tries to dupe others,
he ends up looking like a dope.

115.

The stubborn views of others
are best left untouched.

116.

Crushing blows of intense situations
call for more strength.

In the end, strength is the gift.

117.

Thank your difficult history for
making you strong.

118.

Conquer every challenge, even if
it takes time and grit.

119.

The moment of death is as easy
as walking out the door.

120.

There is a time to be born and
a moment to depart.

Everything is perfect, according to
the soul's plan.

121.

Cherish each moment. Life is a fleeting flash
from birth to the change called death.

122.

When the time is near for passing,
to prolong life is not a favor.

123.

A question: Why do I dwell on
the faults of others?

Reply: Ah, you are dealing with the same issues.

124.

To be pleased with your behavior at the end
of the day is a great triumph.

125.

Observe life and learn from it, but refrain from
judging others in your script.

126.

Refuse to let the hurtful words of others
cause you to subscribe to the erroneous belief
that you are small and insignificant.

127.

Smiles are the universal language of all people.

128.

Smile warmly at everyone, including
your own face in the mirror.

129.

The tongue is quick to speak. In many cases
it is better to remain silent.

130.

Excessive speech wastes the valuable resource
of physical energy.

131.

Choose your words carefully. They can have
a soothing or unsettling effect on others.

132.

Nagging is a bad habit. It is called tailgating
another with your tongue!

133.

Curt comments cut congenial
conversations abruptly.

134.

Let others have the last word if that's their gig.
It doesn't make their opinion true.

135.

You were sharp with me. Ouch! That was
a painful return of my own speech.

136.

Jealousy is a cruel creature
that shows no mercy.

137.

Wild eyes of jealousy cannot be hidden
behind sweet words.

138.

Others may say your plans will not succeed.

Ah, there is no reason to listen to jealous talk.

139.

Life has a big whisk that it uses to blend people together who have similar lessons to learn.

140.

The roller coaster of revenge is guaranteed to be a scream-producing ride.

141.

If you argue with a wrangler, you will get burned with a hot iron of revenge.

142.

The past is the past—old and tired.

The present is a glorious time of opportunity.

143.

One can only rectify the past in the present.

144.

We are thought-creators of a grand
or grouchy tomorrow.

145.

The unhelpful habit of trying
to peer into the future prevents one
from living in the joyful now.

146.

Do each chore well, then put your tools away.

147.

Bottled-up emotions are best
poured down the drain.

148.

To weep for one reason may not be close
to the real reason for tears.

149.

A flash flood of tears is far better than
a stack of stored emotions.

150.

Sadness now may be easier than the pain
of manifested desires.

151.

No matter what others predict,
you are not obligated to fail.

152.

Flexibility makes room for inner guidance
to direct your life.

153.

Let's work on resolving situations
in a win/win way.

154.

It is liberating work to iron out the wrinkles
of your hurt feelings.

155.

The most significant healing happens after
forgiveness has done its splendid work.

156.

Forgive, yet do not stay within someone's
fist-swinging range.

157.

Be soft-spoken with a tough skin
for protection from abusive energies.

158.

Hate is binding until forgiveness releases
the taut cords of negative attachment.

159.

Stealing is never free.

160.

Speak ill of no one, lest the returning voice
of gossip targets you.

161.

Many people focus on the snarl of
human noises. How boring to listen
to who — did — what.

162.

Maneuver around those who want to gossip.

It is best not to get involved in pettiness.

163.

Gossip is violence.

164.

Greedy people cannot hide their grabby fingers beneath white gloves of pure intention.

165.

The greedy are unwittingly laying the foundation for future times as the needy.

166.

Give where it is needed, not where it's desired from a greedy perspective.

167.

Be careful when you are with those of a greedy mentality.

Their behavior is not sincere.

168.

Why must everything be done in one day?

Ah, the galloping mind cannot stop.

169.

Let life evolve at its own pace —
there is no need to rush.

170.

If evil had a face, it would be called ignorance.

171.

Construct a policy to let no one
send you on a guilt trip.

172.

It's time to release that deeply held grudge.
Gently open your fist and let it go.

173.

An incredible amount of energy
is expended to carry a grudge.

174.

Avoiding an issue does not make it go away.

It just gives the unresolved a place to fester in
the mental chamber of unwanted thoughts.

175.

The same theme is played out over and
over again through experiences until we
change our mode of thinking.

176.

Sometimes, our life seems to go into a blender.

We come out a bit shaky, but
always more refined!

177.

Postpone all worries until tomorrow.
Always live in the present.

178.

Walk through open doors.

Choose not to fret about closed doors.

179.

A fond hope: May conflict never
create a nest in your head.

180.

Life often uses a jackhammer to help
us learn our lessons.

181.

What a loud clamor many make
over small matters.

182.

You can deal with a challenge unless
you see it as a monster to slay.

183.

The fiercest battles are fought in the mind.

184.

I love humor. It helps me reboot my cranial
computer when it crashes.

185.

To push someone in a specific direction is sure
to bring stress to the one exerting the pressure.

186.

In the ballgame of life, both happiness
and sorrow take their turn at bat.

187.

The whys of life are best left unasked.

188.

There is no niceness behind fake friendliness.

189.

Look at hardships as a quick way to fracture rigid bits of ignorance.

190.

The musty cellar of attitudes contains some awful stuff.

191.

If you are not willing to change direction, what's the point of having a steering wheel?

192.

Locate negative patterns of thought.

Pull them out like weeds.

Plant positive thoughts and beautiful flowers will grow.

193.

Nothing can be lost unless it is meant to go.

194.

There is a decided difference between being kind and doing nice deeds to obtain favors.

195.

Never tire of pasting beautiful pictures into the photo albums of others' lives.

196.

Everything is perfect, though we may not understand it at the time.

197.

Stay optimistic. It will all work out.

198.

The message of our lives is not written in time, but in the hearts we touch along the way.

199.

Every moment spent in nature's quiet is worth more than a thousand days lived in places of chatter.

200.

We are sunbeams. We dance together for a while and then move on.

201.

Much can be garnered by listening
instead of chattering mindlessly while
others evaluate your sanity.

202.

When we share with others, abundance returns.

203.

Unkind actions directed toward you
should not be stored in you.

204.

The mind likes to flirt with negative creations.

An affirmation holds the mind steady
on a focused point.

205.

Here is a power-packed affirmation:
I am professional in everything I do.

206.

Say to yourself: Today, I will let troublesome
situations glide off my shoulders.

207.

An affirmation: I am a kaleidoscope
of colors, radiating the dazzling light
from The Divine within.

208.

A blessing: May all your needs be met
and your joy be full and complete.

209.

May joy ring throughout our world,
helping peace to abound.

210.

We cannot change others; we can only change
ourselves — and that is full-time work.

211.

Cheerfulness, calmness, and courage are the core qualities needed to navigate life.

212.

A fun project: Send a Cheer-O-Gram (a message) to someone who needs to be uplifted.

213.

Choices bring painful or pleasant returns.

214.

Everyone must earn their rewards.

Everyone must face the consequences of their actions.

215.

There is much pain in the crowd.

Support those who mourn and wipe away
the tears of those who weep.

216.

One compassionate gesture comforts
all grieving people worldwide.

217.

Real estate advice: A high-rise consciousness
is a beautiful place to reside.

218.

The *weak* know they cannot.

The *sometimes strong* believe it is possible.

The *strong* create success with
unwavering determination.

219.

Any food eaten in excess has the potential
to become a poison.

220.

Purchase fresh, organic foods.

Every day eat some fruits and vegetables
in their raw state.

221.

Sugary treats tire the body.

Salty foods create tension.

222.

Determine to be disciplined in all avenues
of your life.

223.

Tread upon the earth with footsteps of respect.

224.

Mother Earth enjoys her rain showers
immensely.

They cool her surface from the steaming
heat of man's intensities.

225.

Spiritual wisdom is the best form of education.

226.

The sweet smiles of wise elders encourage
us to savor our days.

227.

Learn to relax while working,
not just after working.

228.

Be vast! Think outside the box of limitation,
hesitation, and fear.

229.

Visualize an endless sky that is brushed
with morning light.

Merge into this expansive sight.

230.

It is better to have childlike faith than volumes
of dry intellectual knowledge.

231.

Rumbles over supposed slights keep families
erupting with personality steam.

232.

Extract yourself quickly from a family feud.

233.

A loving family is a grand gift.

234.

Trying to placate someone who is demanding
is a never-ending, thankless task.

235.

A happy thought to send to your friends: A soft
place in my heart is reserved for you.

236.

One loses friends quickly by being demanding,
critical, clingy, or unappreciative.

237.

It is better to have a staunch critic to sand your
character than a professed friend who showers
you with ego-building insincerities.

238.

Friends are not always loyal.

Enemies masquerade as friends.

We live in a strange place.

239.

Life sifts false friends through
the sieve of loyalty.

240.

Gentle days come from soft-hearted ways.

241.

Aim to live in a perpetual state of gratitude.

242.

Move away from the debilitating habit
of needing the approval of others.

243.

True happiness is a state of heart.

Pleasure is a passing fantasy.

244.

The inclement weather of surrounding events cannot dim a happy disposition.

245.

For happiness: Lead an uncomplicated life, unwind from troublesome situations, and adopt a positive approach.

246.

There is no need to waste your happy on someone who wants to be a grump!

247.

A formula for happiness: Wish everyone well, even those who would like to see you fail.

248.

Old resentments, kept alive and thriving,
erode the happiness of the holder.

249.

Walk away peacefully from places
where harmony does not exist.

250.

Harmony within and with all people
is the secret to a happy smile.

251.

The mind is the place where
disease is generated.

252.

Many people pray for healing of the physical
body, but neglect to ask for help in healing
the illusions of the mind.

253.

Pickled with the vinegar of bitterness,
many wonder why their bellies ache.

254.

May all my wounds heal.

Forgive me when I have hurt others.

May their wounds heal too.

255.

Healing pain from the past releases the tight
cords of distress that block the circuitry of love.

256.

Rest is an excellent restorative remedy.

257.

Religion aims to bring peace to followers
and the world.

258.

Non-violence, tolerance, truthfulness, and love
are the cornerstones of spiritual thought.

259.

The three major tenets of the spiritual
path: Seek the Divine, live a pure life,
and do good to others.

260.

Unity does not mean having the same
approach to The Divine.

Unity is coming together with love and respect.

261.

Have an open heart toward the
followers of all paths.

262.

Prayers send soft waves of peace
to hurting hearts.

263.

Prayer is our friend on the sometimes
arduous path of life.

264.

Pray to have peace amid chaos,
love when surrounded by hatred, and
the fortitude to remain strong through
the ever-changing scenes of life.

265.

May all people be given the necessities
they need for untroubled living.

266.

Most Effulgent God, help me to release
the knots of tension that I unwittingly created
during times of unwholesome behavior.

267.

It is our soul's service to bring light
into dim places.

268.

We are on a journey to make
the world sparkle again.

269.

Structure your life in ways that bring
the most good to others.

270.

May our combined efforts of selfless service
bring hope and cheer to many hearts.

271.

The peace of nature is a healing herb
that treats many wounds.

272.

May every moment be treasured, every
thought beam skyward, every action be helpful,
and every word be beautiful.

273.

Think of the good, not the troublesome.

Think of the joyful, not the sad.

Think of your possibilities and begin to soar.

274.

Escape from the empty pleasures
of this material-driven world.

Pray and savor silence.

275.

Our arms are trauma centers where
those who suffer can find solace.

276.

Difficult experiences are birthing rooms
for compassion.

277.

Cherish each day.

Time moves on, and scenes change.

278.

Life's lessons help us turn old rust into
pure gold — one speck at a time.

279.

When a fault is healed, we feel clearer.

280.

Take a microscopic view of your character,
then work to cleanse the imperfect.

281.

May the radio station of our hearts always
be tuned to the station of love.

282.

Humility takes us to great places.

283.

May we walk upon the earth with the
divine strength of a roaring lion and
the peace of a gentle lamb.

284.

In all situations, remember to
hold your energy tall.

285.

When we live our lives with warm
regard for people worldwide, a geyser of
limitless joy erupts in our hearts.

286.

Gratitude brings prompt and
wondrous returns.

287.

This world is a fantastic exfoliant
to cleanse our blemishes!

288.

Learn to be comfortable in your skin.

289.

You are a being of light.

290.

Be mild-mannered, approachable,
and optimistic.

291.

Stay on the joyful side of life.

292.

Shine like the sun.

293.

Radiate warmth to all living beings.

294.

Imbibe wisdom; share wisdom.

295.

Do as much good as you can.

296.

You are here at the perfect cosmic
moment to serve.

297.

No one can take your place.

298.

Stay strong; remain hopeful.

299.

Be happy as you learn and grow.

300.

Remember to keep a sense of
humor in your pocket.

301.

Smile on!

Goodbye for now.

We'll be together again soon in the next book.

My love is always with you.

Books by Shanti Rose are available in both print and eBook. The eBook edition showcases a selection of visionary art by Shanti, along with her inspired interpretations.

The parade of books by Shanti Rose has begun. Watch for new titles coming soon.

If you would like to connect with Shanti, you can email her at Shanti@shantiday.com, visit her website at shantiday.com, or send correspondence to the address below.

Shanti Rose
Turquoise River Publications
4315 50th Street NW
Suite 100 PMB 7034
Washington, DC. 20016